AMERICAN ICONS

Statue of Liberty

Steve Goldsworthy

LET'S READ

AV2 BY WEIGL

ADDED VALUE • AUDIO VISUAL

www.av2books.com

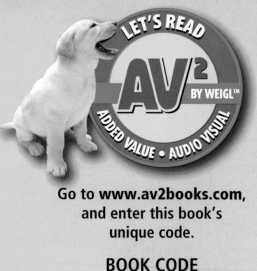

LET'S READ
AV²
BY WEIGL™
ADDED VALUE • AUDIO VISUAL

Go to **www.av2books.com**, and enter this book's unique code.

BOOK CODE

L991506

AV² by Weigl brings you media enhanced books that support active learning.

AV² provides enriched content that supplements and complements this book. Weigl's AV² books strive to create inspired learning and engage young minds in a total learning experience.

Your AV² Media Enhanced books come alive with...

Audio
Listen to sections of the book read aloud.

Video
Watch informative video clips.

Embedded Weblinks
Gain additional information for research.

Try This!
Complete activities and hands-on experiments.

Key Words
Study vocabulary, and complete a matching word activity.

Quizzes
Test your knowledge.

Slide Show
View images and captions, and prepare a presentation.

... and much, much more!

Published by AV² by Weigl
350 5th Avenue, 59th Floor, New York, NY 10118
Website: www.av2books.com   www.weigl.com

Library of Congress Control Number: 2012940128

ISBN 978-1-61913-076-0 (hard cover)
ISBN 978-1-61913-303-7 (soft cover)

Printed in the United States of America in North Mankato, Minnesota
1 2 3 4 5 6 7 8 9 16 15 14 13 12

052012
WEP050412

Editor: Aaron Carr   **Design:** Mandy Christiansen

Photo Credits
Every reasonable effort has been made to trace ownership and to obtain permission to reprint copyright material. The publishers would be pleased to have any errors or omissions brought to their attention so that they may be corrected in subsequent printings.

Weigl acknowledges Getty Images as the primary image supplier for this title.

CONTENTS

What is the Statue of Liberty?

The Statue of Liberty is a well known statue.
It is in New York City. It was built many
years ago.

5

A National Symbol

The Statue of Liberty was a gift from France to the United States. It stands for the friendship between the two countries.

Naming the Statue

People from France named the Statue of Liberty. Liberty means freedom.

10

Statue of Liberty Artists

Statues are made by artists. Many artists worked together to make the Statue of Liberty.

What is the Statue of Liberty Made of?

The Statue of Liberty is made of a metal called copper. The base is made from stone.

13

14

Building the Statue

French workers made the statue. American workers made the base. It took nine years to make the statue.

Where is the Statue of Liberty?

The Statue of Liberty stands on Liberty Island. This small island is in the New York City harbor.

Becoming an Icon

The Statue of Liberty was the tallest structure in New York when it was made. People around the world soon came to see the statue as a symbol of freedom.

The Statue of Liberty Today

Many people visit the Statue of Liberty each year. There are many steps to climb to reach the top. People can look out of the windows in the statue's crown.

STATUE OF LIBERTY FACTS

These pages provide detailed information that expands on the interesting facts found in the book. These pages are intended to be used by adults as a learning support to help young readers round out their knowledge of each national symbol featured in the *American Icons* series.

Pages 4–5

What is the Statue of Liberty? The Statue of Liberty is a famous landmark in New York City. It is also one of the most famous statues in the world. Workers began building the Statue of Liberty in 1875. It was completed in 1884. The statue was dedicated October 28, 1886. It is a symbol of U.S. freedom and independence, and one of the country's most recognizable icons.

Pages 6–7

A National Symbol In 1865, French historian Édouard René de Laboulaye mentioned the idea of building a monument to American independence. French sculptor Frédéric Bartholdi was inspired by his words. He felt the U.S. history of revolution and independence was similar to French history. The monument would become a symbol of friendship between the two countries.

Pages 8–9

Naming the Statue The official name of the statue is "Liberty Enlightening the World." Frédéric Bartholdi named the statue. He also designed the statue. He based his designs for the statue on many things. The face is thought to be based on Bartholdi's own mother. The body was designed to represent Libertas, the Roman goddess of freedom.

Pages 10–11

Statue of Liberty Artists Frédéric Bartholdi studied fine art and architecture in France. He created many works of art, including a fountain in Washington, D.C., and the "Lion of Belfort," a gigantic lion carved into the side of a mountain in Belfort, France. In 1922, a museum of his work was founded in Colmar, France.

Pages 12–13

What is the Statue of Liberty Made of? Workers hammered hundreds of giant copper sheets over wooden molds of the statue. The copper pieces were mounted over a skeleton-like structure made of iron and steel. In 1885, the statue was taken apart, packed into 214 crates, and shipped to New York. The statue is 151 feet (46 m) high. It was the tallest statue in the world at the time.

Pages 14–15

Building the Statue French and American workers built the Statue of Liberty. The French built the statue in France, while Americans built the pedestal in New York. The statue was taken apart, transported, and reassembled in the United States. French engineer Alexandre-Gustave Eiffel and structural engineer Maurice Koechlin built the statue's "skeleton" frame. Eiffel later built the Eiffel Tower.

Pages 16–17

Where is the Statue of Liberty? In June 1871, Frédéric Bartholdi traveled to the U.S. to discuss designs for the statue. As he arrived at New York Harbor, he passed the tiny Bedloe's Island. He thought it would make a perfect spot for the Statue of Liberty. He visited President Ulysses S. Grant and learned the island was owned by the government. In 1956, the name of the island was changed to Liberty Island.

Pages 18–19

Becoming an Icon The Statue of Liberty is 305 feet (93 meters) tall. The statue holds a torch high in the air as a symbol of freedom for all people. The tablet the statue carries has July 4, 1776, written on it. This is the date the U.S. Declaration of Independence was signed. For immigrants to the United States, the statue represented a better life. To others, it represented independence and freedom.

Pages 20–21

The Statue of Liberty Today More than five million people visit the Statue of Liberty each year. Visitors can climb 354 steps to reach the observation deck in the statue's crown. A plaque at the entrance displays the poem *The New Colossus* by Emma Lazarus. It contains the famous words, "Give me your tired, your poor, your huddled masses yearning to breathe free." Many people feel these words summarize the ideals the Statue of Liberty is meant to represent.

KEY WORDS

Research has shown that as much as 65 percent of all written material published in English is made up of 300 words. These 300 words cannot be taught using pictures or learned by sounding them out. They must be recognized by sight. This book contains 44 common sight words to help young readers improve their reading fluency and comprehension. This book also teaches young readers several important content words, such as nouns. These words are paired with pictures to aid in learning and improve understanding.

Page	Sight Words First Appearance
4	a, city, in, is, it, many, the, was, well, what, years
7	between, for, from, to, two
8	means, named, people
11	are, by, made, make, together
12	of
15	American, took
16	on, small, this, where
19	an, around, as, came, see, soon, when, world
21	can, each, look, out, there

Page	Content Words First Appearance
4	New York, statue, Statue of Liberty
7	countries, France, friendship, gift, symbol, United States
8	freedom, liberty
11	artists
12	base, copper, metal, stone
15	workers
16	harbor, island, Liberty Island
19	icon, structure
21	crown, steps, top, windows